MW00714997

THE WOMEN WHO LOVED ELVIS ALL THEIR LIVES

Other Books by Fleda Brown

Breathing In, Breathing Out (poems)
The Devil's Child (poems)*
The Earliest House (chapbook, poems)*
Do Not Peel the Birches (poems)*
Fishing With Blood (poems)*
Critical Essays on D. H. Lawrence (co-edited)*

*as Fleda Brown Jackson

THE WOMEN WHO LOVED ELVIS ALL THEIR LIVES

poems by
Fleda Brown

CARNEGIE MELLON UNIVERSITY PRESS

Pittsburgh 2004

ACKNOWLEDGMENTS

Some poems in this collection have previously appeared in the following journals:

Arts and Letters, "Tillywilly Fog" (as "Sestina for Elvis")
Artful Dodge, "Elvis Reads the Story of the Woman at the Well"
American Poetry Review, "Bus Stop"
Crab Orchard Review, "The Jungle Room," "Shaking Hands With
 Nixon" (as "Elvis Shaking Hands With Nixon"), "The
 Original Sun Recording"
Georgia Review, "Elvis Sings Gospel"
Iowa Review, "Elvis Goes to the Army," "The Women Who Loved Elvis
 All Their Lives," "The Death of Gladys Presley," "The
 Twenty-Four Hour Church of Elvis"
Kestrel, The "Graceland" series
Poetry, "Elvis Reads 'The Wild Swans at Coole,'" "Industrial Teflon
 Comes into Use for Kitchen Pots and Pans"
Shenandoah, "Country" (as "Country Music")
West Branch, "I Escape With My Mother in the DeSoto"
Yarrow, "Elvis Acts as His Own Pallbearer"

The "Graceland" poems won the 1999 *Kestrel* Writing Contest. "Elvis Reads
'The Wild Swans at Coole,'" "Elvis Sings Gospel," "Elvis Goes to the Army,"
"Elvis Acts as His Own Pallbearer," "Elvis at the End of History," "The
Women Who Loved Elvis All Their Lives," and "The Death of Gladys Presley"
have been reprinted in *Elvis Poems: Twentieth-Century Poets on a Cultural Icon,*
ed. Will Clemens, University of Arkansas Press, 2001.

I am very grateful to Jeanne Murray Walker, Andrea Hollander Budy, Lola
Haskins, Cruce Stark, Enid Shomer, Julianna Baggott, and Jerry Beasley for
their help at various stages of this manuscript. Many thanks to Anne Lorton
for the cover photograph.

The publication of this book is made possible by a grant from
the Pennsylvania Council on the Arts.

Book design: Sarah Smith
Library of Congress Control Number: 2003103588
ISBN 0-88748-403-4
Printed and bound in the United States of America

10 9 8 7 6 5 4 3 2 1

CONTENTS

This book is for
Jerry, Steve, Vic, George, John, and Bruce—
my favorite rock & roll band, Jerry and the Juveniles—

I
THE ORIGINAL SUN RECORDING

THE ORIGINAL SUN RECORDING

What is coming has to wait
until the mind quits looking. I am trying not to watch this poem.
I am trying like hell to keep track of Elvis
to follow him on the other side of the sound booth glass.

It is late, after their regular jobs,
hot as a sweat lodge in the sound booth.
They have tried dozens of tunes.
Sam Phillips stands off, making suggestions.

A poem has to be glass.
I know that, Robert Francis.
I know that, Julian of Norwich. I know that, Gautama Siddhartha.
Elvis on one side, me on the other.
I bring the saints in to help me make my words invisible.

I ask them to give me a curve ball, something unexpected,
that looks like a screw-up. I remind them how easily
they have flown through physics, story line, musical notation.

What keeps Elvis and me going is
we don't know whether to laugh or cry.
When the music takes off, it is almost grief.
He tries the old blues song, "That's All Right, Mama,"
He starts jumping around like a kid, wiggling his leg.
Bill Black starts pretending his bass is a pogo stick.
You can hear Sam at the end of the original cut,
his astonished whoop.

TILLYWILLY FOG

I'm kissing his poster, on my knees on my bed.
We're both children, in a way. Maybe we stop
at fifteen. We could easily be in the fogged-
up car at Tillywilly Quarry. We haven't, you know,
yet. It begins here. The rest seems like a vast
openness. I cannot imagine past his hand

up my skirt any more than he could imagine handing
back his songs to silence, or lying on his death-bed
without Priscilla or Kathy or Linda or Jo or vast
numbers of other girls called in to stop
his mind enough so he could sleep. What we know
together is half-shut eyes, call it a fog

of desire, if you want, but there is something in the fog
that is not us, an alertness of mind, a hand
running over the entirety of what we know
and calling it good. No matter whose bed
you get in later, something in your mind stops
here: you and Elvis touch lips across the vast

distance. Don't sap this up: the truth is vaster
than the jewel-belted icon stumbling in a fog
of barbiturates. The vibration of the universe never stops.
It's all song, the hum of molecules in the hand
and lips, and what goes away comes back, a flower-bed
of humming, spilling over the edge of what you know.

You think the fat women who cried didn't know
what they cried for, when he died? It's no vast
distance between them and me. Our souls are bedded
in our hungry bodies, taking advantage of the fog
at Tillywilly. "Please let me put my hand
there," he says, and being scared, he stops

there. Nothing ever felt this good, to stop
on that note, the mouth wide open, no
thought left, no design, waiting for the hand
of God to move on or intervene. It's vastness,
it's plenty, it's human spring, pure song, a fog
of wastefulness. You get out of bed

the rest of your life knowing it's Elvis's bed
you've come from—vast, vibrating. On the one hand,
you're stopped, flesh and bone; on the other, you're a song.

COLLAR TURNED UP LIKE ELVIS'S

He could hold up the wall
in his black jacket, fill his eyes
with her pearl-studded sweater, until
there was no namby-pamby basketball game
left, nothing but his steamed-up
Buick windows, "Bird Dog"
on K-HOG forever.

      He could get her to drink
a tall Schlitz before noon,
so she would sink through the day as if
it were a bed of leaves, ending up
at the Dixie Cream Donut Shop
where his mother was turning a flotilla
of inner tubes, lifting them screen
by screen, zipping glaze across.

      He could leave his cigarette
on the American eagle ashtray,
go back for a drag: pillar of smoke,
pillar of fire. He could kiss his mother
like an angry lover, the mother who was
punching donuts over with a stick,
catching them on the edge, no dent
for grease to get in. He could allow
the girlfriend to turn them,
soaking up grease, while his dad,
a little drunk, whistled "Cherry Pink
and Apple Blossom White"
in the back room.

        Mostly, the boyfriend
could say for sure which one
had waited for the other by the gym,
which of them was utterly dissolute
with the moment that was coming,
that would be, yes, like sinking a shot
that never touched the rim, nothing
to hold onto.
        It wasn't him.

ELVIS ARON AND JESSE GARON

"When one twin died, the one that lived got all
the strength of both," their mother Gladys liked
to say, and that remnant of a son would pluck at her voice,
the little dread in every pleasure, and Elvis
would quiver on the stage of her thoughts, and she would kiss him
on the lips, and he would kiss her back, and let her
take him to her bosom until it felt like the other son
joined with this one, and Elvis could leave her again,
carrying away the seed of worry and decay
that never had a voice. On camera, then,
he would seem to cock his head to listen,
shock of hair over one eye. He would take
Delores Hart into his arms, and we could almost
hear the dark child sigh in its dream of being born.

VISITING VERNON IN PARCHMAN PRISON

It was five hours on the Greyhound.
You needed to get cleaned up in Tutwiler
before the last twenty minutes down to Parchman.
There's a thin line between respectable and not.
You had to have your dress starched, hair slicked,
walk right up to the man and say, "I'm Mrs. Presley,
here to see my husband. This is his son."

She would sit down
and say, "Tell your daddy what you been doing,"
and he would recite as if he were in school,
mother and son on the same side of the bars
as the Assembly of God church,
holding hands.
They didn't put him there, did they?
They didn't forge the check.
Still, there was the effort to do all the talking,
not to talk baby-talk between themselves.

MEMPHIS DISCOVERS ELVIS

She hears her son's name
over and over, "That's All Right"
played eleven times.
Memphis sits by the radio
while he's gone to see Autry
in *Goldtown Ghost Riders*.

If you're going to have a famous son,
you already know before it happens,
but still, it seems as if they're saying
he died, instead of what they do say—

this boy who used to sit on the curb
at the corner of Main in a sailor hat,
bright and earnest, but oh!
the city flinging itself into him even then.
Who could say when the awful
moment would be, when the child
would step off into one particular song
as if into heavy traffic?

Too late to save him now.
Gladys and Vernon rush down
opposite aisles of the movies.
Nothing to do but get him out of there
and down to WHBQ.
Tell him the disk jockey wants him
to recall as best he can
his mortal life, on air.

IF I CAN DREAM

He's alone in the sound booth, recording "If I Can Dream,"
full orchestra in the headphones.
He wants the hand-held mike, not the boom.
He wants the lights dimmed.
Second take, he's sitting on the linoleum floor.
Third take, he's lying on his back, lights off.
Then, my God, he's in the fetal position in total darkness.

I'm with you, King. You won't get out of the world that way,
but I like to watch you try.
You don't care if you're crazy or not.
You just let the dark sing you back from its brink
every second.
And when the lights come on
and you sheepishly dust off your pants,
I want to say: don't worry, the dark still loves you.
It's caught in your hair and under your eyes.
No matter how fast you move,
look, it's holding on.

ELIVS GOES TO THE ARMY

"Goodby, you long black sonofabitch," he says
to his limo as he climbs on the bus to basic training.
The U.S. Army has him on the scales, then,
in his underpants, baby fat showing, mouth downturned
in sorrow or fear. It is worth noting when a person
chooses to leave his mama and his singing behind,
gives over to the faint signals picked up by his inner ear.
So what if the signal in a particular case is mundane:
the unremarkable desire for clarity, for love.
He's more alert than he's ever been, time clicking
away with the greater ritual's small appointments:
dressing and undressing, tightening bedcovers, reciting
the valuable gun, becoming part of the diorama
where danger is everywhere, a good reason to blend
khaki with the earth.
                    Now, thirty years later, uniforms
are back in favor, following the lead of Catholic
children in navy and white, soldiers of God
and high-scorers on SATs alike, sure
of their place in the universe. "This is the Army, son":
even a King like Elvis might hear that
and relax at last between what's come before
and what will be: the dead hair of the past
buzzed off in a second, a battalion of stubs that hope
to live up to the example of the fallen. We will not laugh
at the shorn head, but will consider a long time
the incomprehensibility of our desires, and the way
we beg ritual to take them off our hands.

THE DEATH OF GLADYS

The doctor put her on a "soft diet," then,
which she interpreted as Pepsi-Cola and watermelon,
but that didn't kill her, her liver did,
and when it was over, the wild excesses
of grief you might have guessed: "Look at them hands,
Oh God, those hands toiled to raise me," bringing
in the Bible word *toiled* for added weight.
The kind of grief it's hard to believe in,
from the outside, it seems to delight so in the show.
"Elvis, look at them chickens. Mama ain't
never gonna feed them chickens no more,"
Vernon said, picking out objects to reverence
for their recent lostness. It's the truth, though,
the way Elvis touched things, then, with handfuls of fire,
and the way the wind hit his face as the celestial
door opened and the voice that had been in secret
between mother and son shone tremendously,
at that moment, before death finished penetrating
her body, feet last. "Look at her little sooties,
she's so precious," Elvis cried, leaning over the coffin
and hugging and kissing her feet, then her hands and face
until they had to cover her in glass, the one
pure object waiting to be raised. "Everything I have
is gone," he cried, and this was the truth, poor child
made of practically all suffering, having to
come back to it over and over to get it right.

II
BETWEEN THRUST AND GRAVITY

ELVIS READS THE STORY OF THE WOMAN AT THE WELL

He is reading the Bible to the scantily-clad girls
draped on his armchair,
each selected to his specifications—
none having borne a child, none older than twenty.
The book on his open hand is a flailing bird
tethered to his darker self.
Anyone who had had a twin that died
might always be checking to find out "Which one am I?"
Look at him drumming his fingers on the Bible,
one twin restless inside the other.

One of the girls winds her leg around his
and asks, "Was the woman at the well a virgin, Elvis?"
(This is after the part where Jesus says clearly
about the five husbands.)

How carefully, how seemingly reluctantly, he's learned
to coax the dark self upward in these situations,
to get a thousand girls screaming
the Samaritan woman's words:
        "Sir, give me the water that ends all thirst,"

to see his Bible self
on the other side of the lights, grabbing
for the sweaty scarf thrown
from the stage,
knowing he could be the one
who gets to be comforted forever.

THE WOMEN WHO LOVED ELVIS
ALL THEIR LIVES

She reads, of course, what he's doing, shaking Nixon's hand,
dating this starlet or that, while he is faithful to her
like a stone in her belly, like the actual love child,
its bills and diapers. Once he had kissed her
and time had stood still, at least some point seems to
remain back there as a place to return to, to wait for.
What is she waiting for? He will not marry her, nor will he
stop very often. Desireé will grow up to say her father is dead.
Desireé will imagine him standing on a timeless street,
hungry for his child. She will wait for him, not in the original,
but in a gesture copied to whatever lover she takes.
He will fracture and change to landscape, to the Pope, maybe,
or President Kennedy, or to a pain that darkens her eyes.

"Once," she will say, as if she remembers,
and the memory will stick like a fishbone. She knows
how easily she will comply when a man puts his hand
on the back of her neck and gently steers her.
She knows how long she will wait for rescue, how the world
will go on expanding outside. She will see her mother's photo
of Elvis shaking hands with Nixon, the terrifying conjunction.
A whole war with Asia will begin slowly,
in her lifetime, out of such irreconcilable urges.
The Pill will become available to the general public,
starting up a new waiting in that other depth.
The egg will have to keep believing in its timeless moment
of completion without any proof except in the longing
of its own body. Maris will break Babe Ruth's record
while Orbison will have his first major hit with
"Only the Lonely," trying his best to sound like Elvis.

PRISCILLA PRESLEY, 1962

She is grateful for how
the little world of Graceland
holds her in, teaches her to give up
the small self to the universal good.
She is watching him for clues,
what moves he responds to.
She learned at fifteen to keep her mind
ahead of his. She dyed her hair black,
like his. She is aware of a feeling
of constant swooning, as if she were
on her knees, and after she complains
about Anita, or Ann-Margret, the sheets
still warm from one of them, she is
literally on her knees, begging him
to stop raging, stop throwing lamps
and chairs, not to send her back
to Germany. It feels like love
at its most pure—whelmed
with longing—drawing out of her
the noblest of efforts. Often the fights
seem not like fights at all,
but like opposite muscles of the same
flesh. As if she is raging against
her own self until she sobs,
and is light enough to float again
on the river of his desires.
Then he is straightening the lamp,
picking up the chair, and kissing her,
and it is all right now, though
there was always the chance,
will always be the chance. . . .
        After that, the whole gang,
she and the Memphis boys, go out
on the lawn to watch the King
light his cigar, fly his toy plane.

ELVIS DECIDES TO BECOME A MONK

Because he has been reading *Autobiography of a Yogi*,
The Leaves of Maya's Garden, and Krishnamurti's *The First and
                                                    Last Freedom.*
Because he has been meditating and has stopped having sex,
and because he has prayed for months
for a clear sign which finally in the desert on the way to L.A.
revealed itself as Joseph Stalin in the clouds,
which was about his more evil self,
so he surrendered himself among the Joshua trees
and his heart was pierced, and when it exploded
he saw the face of Christ and the truth of existence.

Because this life of hotel rooms and limousines
is already a monastery,
every human contact a mirror in the face.
Because Delores Hart became a nun.
Because the Assembly of God preacher taught him better than
this life—
not this Elvis Presley but the plain boy
God shaped out of the earth like a saguaro cactus.
Because he has pressed his precious guitar-playing hands
against the cactus spines to ground at last the pain
that has been flying through the air
like lightning bolts.

SHAKING HANDS WITH NIXON

Otherwise, Elvis would be crashing against
the walls of the Oval Office, confused bird
in silver-plated amber-tinted designer sunglasses
and purple cape,
high-collar shirt open halfway to the waist.

He is trying to get things under control.
Joplin and Hendrix have just died of drugs.
Uncle Johnny's died of drink; Cousin Bobby's swallowed rat poison.

Elvis has brought Nixon gifts, a fistful of deputy badges
from his personal collection,
and a picture of Priscilla and Lisa Marie,
even though Priscilla's just walked out on him.
He has come to ask Nixon for a Federal Bureau of Narcotics badge.
He has done an "in-depth study of drug abuse,"
particularly among Beatles fans.
He's worried about the Beatles making all that money and taking it
                                        to England.
He tells Nixon they may be un-American.
He tells Nixon about his gun collection.

He tries to get across that he knows the awful changes
the country can make when you're not looking,
how one moment can desert the other
and leave you standing in the footlights,
trying to remember if you're supposed to shoot or fly.

SPUTNIK, 1957

Remember the upswing, the peak of the swing
      from the catalpa tree where your stomach paused
              in perfect equilibrium
between thrust and gravity? To get that far and hold it

all around the world, to orbit like the Russians!
      In retrospect: to keep being ten, before,
              well, you know
what followed, what junior high was like: the cold mornings

when your little Silvertone clock-radio clicked on
      a moon in the still-dark sky you had to enter,
              both feet
on the cold floor, one focus of the day's ellipse,

of the fancy bluffing you practiced how to do
      out there, the other you still holding on,
              cold feet slightly
turned out, a hard little bow of feet. The world

split into here and there. Remember, too,
      your Vassarette training bra, your awful
              tantrum, the way
you threw it across the room after one day's

straightjacketing? How loose the Russians had gotten,
      you thought, how lifted, how barely held
              on America's string!
How definitely you would rather be Red than Dead.

THE HISTORY OF ROCK AND ROLL

I
Country

Sometimes I feel so lean
I can get past without brushing the sides.
I am on my first husband's grandparents' farm
in the Ozark valley, valley of mist,
cows nudging the fence,

three-mattress bed on the porch.
When I loved him for that one day.
When we listened in the evening to Jimmie Rodgers
singing "The Soldier's Sweetheart," fattening

his lyrics with patter, "Play that thing,"
or "Hey, hey, it won't be long now,"
his blue yodel like a train across the valley,
like a heartbeat, amplified by your vocal cords
in your sleep.

When we woke to a dream of biscuits
like clouds on top of eggs and bacon, the slick
of molasses, the body soaking up maudlin
fat and sugar the way it soaked up

the old homeplace, the way it made me say,
"How handsome you are, my love, in this iron
bedstead under the weight of old quilts
and breakfast clanking in there." Before

the future cracked its sharp eye open
and light from the kitchen syncopated with rain
on the tin roof, and I am not really there,
but in a caricature of memory, singing

along, having a good time making myself
teary-eyed, rolling the song out of my mouth,
repeating the chorus, moving past it,
with my trim, sexy body.

II
Gospel

The picture of Elvis late at night at the piano,
singing gospel. Everyone has left. There are a few
folding chairs and the upright piano. Elvis
is lifting almost out of his black-and-white shoes;
there's no music to look at. It's so simple, the way
loneliness sits down in the middle of a bare room
and the middle gives way, and here you are, in the real
music that meant itself to be played. He is leaning
to the keys, bringing them to whatever the point was—
the typical point of getting washed in the blood of the Lamb,
or building a sure foundation, or going home
to the Lord—but he is hearing the words as exactly themselves,
individual, no reference to anything. I am not
imagining this. I know it: the way the words
save you by themselves, the hush of the word's entrance
like a spirit-lamp. Nobody wants anything
more than they want *home*—what *home* means—
struck like a gong against itself, reverberating
Gladys, maybe, or Uncle Vester, the Assembly of God
Church, Mississippi Slim, Big Mama Thornton,
Ernest Tubb, all the way out to the barely audible
crowds, the great weariness to come. But inside
is the word, encouraged slightly into music, taking
the shape of the room until neither one exists
any more, doesn't have to, since it is home already.

III
Blues

It's not easy to sing the blues, TVs wedged
in every corner, sound turned off, so you
glance up from time to time, barely a skip
in the conversation at hand. Easy to slide your eyes
from image to image. On MTV, for example,
she's out the door and another Technicolor world blooms—
a sequence of doors, knives, scarves.
She's forgotten leaving him already. Where's the ache
in that? She recalls the heavy breathing, like bellows,
the lean-to of romance falling, that's about it.
        Singing the blues, she'd remember
everything; she'd complain. She'd want
the lights down while she consulted the dream
that's propelled her all these years, her reason
for living. She would definitely not move on. She'd refuse
to grow restless under the magnificent load
of her past, even when it makes her tremble
and run her hands through her hair. It might be
three in the morning, she'd be on chapter five
of her story, and happiness would come riding in
like a younger brother on a scooter, ignorant of the ways
of the world. "Please let me come," he'd beg.
"Okay," she'd say, out of sympathy for his
to-be-broken heart, for his full-time career
of remembering, all of this trailing him
like a wake.

IV
Rock and Roll

If you feel like looking at why things turned out this way.
If he hadn't become a doctor and married the florist's daughter.
If you had risen from the bottom bleacher
and taken his hand and danced to "Unchained Melody,"
if he had asked you, if you had worn decent socks,
if it had not rained on the church hayride,
if he had even put his arm on your shoulder.
If your father had not dumped the interior
of the old Zenith console radio on the living room floor
five minutes before he picked you up for the dance.
If he had not said during history class
that the body is the temple of the holy spirit
when you had already taken up smoking
in the field behind your house.
If you had not learned how to make smoke rings
with your tongue like little atom bombs.
If you had believed in Ricky more than Elvis.

Some say the soul is as light as smoke
and can get away that easily,
convert to a different life.
So you kept lying in the grass with your transistor radio,
drumming yourself to the ground,
in case.

I ESCAPE WITH MY MOTHER
IN THE DESOTO

Listen, it will be all right. I'll drive. Goodby
Maxwell Street, we'll say as if we had a secret
emergency, goodby Bendix spindryer, goodby
petticoats on the line dripping liquid starch.

What's the right phrase you've been looking for
all these years, spitting your morning phlegm?
I think it's Fluid Drive, that revolutionary automatic
kick of the DeSoto into third gear at 45. Exempt

at last from the science of shifting that makes us
both weep! I can get this thing up to 70, flat,
in the stretch by the agri farm—
used to scare starlings out of trees, doing that.

They lift up now, brittle as leaves as we pass,
get past. "Your Father—," you start in as if he were
in the trunk, but then you open a Pepsi. We are
watching him dry up and die away like an argument.

You have worn your pink flowered shorts
and it is as cool as the basement on a hot day,
and Arthur Godfrey has not yet fired Julius LaRosa.
It is as if we are down there listening to the radio,

knees pulled up on the brand clean chenille bedspread.
We are going through *Ladies' Home Journals* and you
are a beauty queen, safe in your vault of clichés,
safe from having to explain anything you mean.

BUS STOP

You are scratching your foot
against the steel leg of the bus seat,
imagining yourself a woman free on the road,
cornfield after cornfield.
You are seventeen and returning to the town
your father's failure took you from,
returning to your old boyfriend
to tie things up so tightly
a whole lifetime cannot untie them.
You picture him encased in his Buick
like a dark spool, his mind turning over
and over, winding you toward him.
After dark, though, you let your head droop
against the soldier from Chicago
on his way to Ft. Chaffee. He
and his friends speak softly, the click
and mumble of their voices naming
guns and machines while you lean on his
khaki, move on out with the infantry,
face the open-mouthed cannon

       which is only the neon flash
of the Iron Skillet bus stop in Centralia,
where you and the soldier are sitting
on stools, smoking and talking over
your separate futures as if the talk
were already betrayal,
your heart lurching awfully easily
into this happiness of riders, his pale mouth
at the center. You hunker
in his mouth to get near your heart.
Out there someone looks up—a small, wild
dishevelment. It is your reflection
in the bus window. You are back
on the bus, are you? All right, then.
you curl up alone on a seat, stuck with
your original plan, too dangerous
a person for anything else.

INDUSTRIAL TEFLON COMES INTO USE FOR KITCHEN POTS AND PANS

After the wars were over, the ones people sang about,
things quit sticking. My grandparents, for instance,
shook the dirt from their shoes and moved to town,
drove the paved streets of Columbia, spurned
orange juice for astronaut Tang.
And what year exactly did I start shaking off hugs?

For a wedding gift, I got Teflon pans.
Teflon, if you'd like to know, is a long-chain polymer,
a fluorocarbon plastic, like Freon.
As good as gold and platinum at resisting things.
Eggs slide right off, as on TV.
Not to mention what came after, Reagan and Bush,
facts sliding across the screen, disappearing
out of memory.
Not to mention the literary canon: Pope, Richardson,
Dryden, Spenser. Who reads them now?

The private name he used to call me, what was it?
The last time, he came through snow, bringing
a bottle of Mateus, and we made love
on the floor, not looking at each other,
nothing left but flesh and bones.
It was 1973, still no news of the danger of Freon.
All summer, I kept the air conditioner on.
The kids opened and closed doors, hot and cold,
the holes in their hearts forming already.
Surely my own mother must have held me, early on,
before I recognized her broken heart and turned away.
Surely her own mother must have held her,
sometimes, in spite of garden-smudged hands,
just to hold her.

III
24-HOUR CHURCH OF ELVIS

ELVIS ACTS AS HIS OWN PALLBEARER

Life up to now had been no mistake,
getting out of East Tupelo,
out of the sharecropper's shack.
Fame was nice.
But this is America,
where you keep redeeming yourself
by leaving the past behind.

It wasn't him in the coffin; anyone could tell
it was a wax dummy. The hair was coming loose,
nose too pug.

How many times had he disappeared
like a magician?
He used to get the body shaking,
the left leg wiggling,
then half-sneer, turn away
from the audience as if he were kidding,

as if he were shaking them off.
We saw how it was done.
You had to make up the moves every day
of your life, start over so many times
you were obvious,
completely American, almost invisible,
so you could leave again,
carry yourself out to the garden
and see what came up next.

DEAD ELVIS

Because he is not visible to the ordinary eye, Elvis
is bench-pressing 250 pounds, turning his belly
to solid iron. He lifts the weight bar
above the second rung. "One more. Be a hero!" He says
to himself what he hears the others say. Baltimore WXBM
is on the radio: Lopez and Bill have just called up
a woman who has vowed to make love to 245 men
in one hour, to break the Guiness record. On the air,
they ask her how, and why, while Elvis is trying to build
a body out of nothing. Get the body Yankee-hard first,
worry about the rest later, he thinks.

The smell of Chinese take-out wafts through
the free-weight room, and he feels himself slipping
out of himself, again, no longer a body, but a hunger.
He pumps the weights, going u-u-u-Huh-Huh-Huh, a-a-h-h-
E-E-E, the way you break through to flesh.
He is tired of being dead, of standing in line at the sub-shop
while others get waited on. His mouth feels like lead,
that much he's got already. Weights clang:
he could be a horse bearing a dead rider
through the town, spurs idly banging his flanks. But
like they say, it's never too late. He is trying not
to think of the Baltimore woman screwing five men
at once, trying not to think of sweet and sour chicken,
but saying Elvis, Elvis, over and over, trying
to hear his mamma say it, back when he was alive.

THE NIGHT BEFORE HER THIRD MARRIAGE, SHE WATCHES A RERUN OF ELVIS'S COMEBACK PERFORMANCE

The night before her third marriage,
she arranges flowers, watches reruns:
he forgets "Heartbreak Hotel"—clutches

his throat—"Worst job I've ever done,"
he says. She loves his failure like she loves
her own skin. She loves his fear,

his one-of-a-kind black leather jumpsuit
over it. She loves whatever protection
there is. Elvis reads his cues

aloud: "Things to talk about"—*First
record, when first met musicians,
Ed Sullivan Show, shooting from waist up.*

Pulls his finger over his curling lip.
While he has her laughing, he's gradually
relaxing away from the past, toward

where he is now, the stool he's sitting on.
He's closing his eyes, going on
with the songs, courting the front row.

She watches for the moment, now,
knowing, from the future, how backstage
after the first set, he called

the costume designer to dry out
the inside of his suit, which he had come in.
She wouldn't want to say how hard she's

watching to see the moment of coming.
He jabs his hand straight up, shouts
"Moby Dick!" and spears the whale. Now.

Or when he leans into the girl's face as if
she already planned to leave him,
so he sends her all he has. It would be

something, to catch what was missed before,
to get in synch with him. It would make
a kind of opening between them, through which

you could fill the past with shaken blossoms.

MRS. LOUISE WELLING SPOTS ELVIS AT HARDING'S MARKET

I felt like I was seeing fireflies—getting little glints,
you know, of what's behind the regular.
Maybe it was the rivets on his suit,
the sunset beaming in the picture window of Harding's Market.
I was standing in line with a full cart,
ice cream for my grandkids, bread for the freezer, etcetera.
He was in front of me, head ducked under,
hair flopping, paying four dollars for fuses, I think.
He had on a white motorcycle suit,
helmet on the counter.
I've never been much of an Elvis fan,
but when you see someone, you know who it is.
Nothing to say about it.
What would I have gained, saying anything?
Put fireflies in a jar—you've got bugs
in a jar, dull tails flashing now and then.
When you drive down a road, though, through fireflies,
they look like an eye opening as you pass between.
I wasn't surprised he was alive.
My nephew getting married—that surprised me.
But Elvis—once a person's all over in movies and records,
I don't think he knows when to stop.
I wouldn't go for a ride on his motorcycle if he asked me.
But when I came out and he was gone, my feet hurt
and I felt tired, useless, like I've always
been going toward something I can't ever get to.

MRS. LOUISE WELLING'S DAUGHER LINDA NEVER SEES ELVIS, BUT BELIEVES

I asked the maintenance man, "Who let you in?"
"Your boyfriend," he said, but I didn't have one.
I knew who it was let him in.
A few days later, there was a note on my windshield:
>   *My dearest Linda, you're a beautiful young lady.*
>   *Someday you'll be my little princess. E. P.*

It takes a burden off Mama, I think,
to have both of us knowing he's out there.
I can't make up to her what she's missed,
herself. My brother who died. And her miscarriage
on the sofa. I'm the oldest of the five, so I helped
clean it up. She never said what it was.

All she did was put up vegetables in jars
in the basement that fall,
fill a few of the empty shelves. Then Daddy left.

Until Elvis, the hardest thing for me was figuring out
where any of this was going.
I bumped along like a rowboat adrift,
scraping against things.

After I had Jake, the nurse came in to tell me
Elvis called. "Make sure she gets the finest of care,"
he said. It wasn't his child of course.
He never interferes.
He's spread out like a net
over my whole life, connecting the dots,
so to speak. I fully expect when I get to the end,
I will be able to read backwards to understand
all that's gone before. It's this I want Mama to hear:
I know it will make sense to us then.

I VISIT THE TWENTY-FOUR HOUR COIN-OP CHURCH OF ELVIS

Portland, Oregon

Well, sure, it's only
a window in a brick wall,
and eight small, seven large, circular framed Elvis-faces
that spin when you put fifty cents in.
The computer screen asks you what you want: wedding,
                                    confession, or what.
I got my personal Elvis I.D. card:
The bearer of this card is a SAINT in the Church of Elvis.
He or she may also be Elvis. Please treat them
accordingly. Thank you.
The faces were spinning like 45s
and I was combing my hair in the plastic reflections,
fixing my lipstick. It was a subtle change.
I think I am probably Elvis. I have begun to feel like
a lost child in Portland, anyway,
to feel uncertainty about my life,
to feel a religious determination to make my words sing.
I was crossing Banning Road to meet you here for lunch,
keeping my hips loose, my sunglasses on.
Didn't I order a cheeseburger for the first time in years?
And I feel I am gradually being purified
of my irony,
back to the true rock and roll.
I want to run my fingers through what hair you have left
and call you Baby, throatily,
and mean for you to Treat Me Accordingly.
We could do our wedding vows again.
I feel we could get all the way back to the original vows,
before our separate cosmic fractures,
the vows we made years ago to other people
that had no irony whatsoever,
that were all Love Me Tender, all Heartbreak Hotel.

ELVIS READS "THE WILD SWANS AT COOLE"

During the First International Elvis Conference in Oxford,
Mississippi, Elvis, alive as ever, is asked to read aloud
"The Wild Swans at Coole," to see what a Hunk

-a Hunk-a Burnin' Love could do to expose the other,
more subtle, longings to the average citizen who might
be raised to contemplate a little, for God's sake,

instead of falling into a blind beat, producing unwanted
babies and maudlin tears! Elvis fingers the page,
tries to plan what to do, sick to death without the music's

jingo, the strings that drive it, and the lyrics that fasten
to the music and ride on through, so the body can be
the words. Meanwhile, they wait for their poem.

He starts at the first, trees in their autumn beauty,
nine-and-fifty swans that take off, or don't, so what?
Among the rows of wan faces, nothing for the thoughts

to take off on, nothing to ease the thoughts. Poem
clamoring on instead of a song, words that aren't supposed
to be said Southern, lines that end before you're finished

thinking, and the last question breaking through the levee
at the end of the lines. He thinks what to do, then, with
his naked and weightless body. They are listening as if

they had got the secret of life into the poem, now,
even with him flying off the end of it, trying to swagger,
one hand in his pocket, bravely cocking an eyebrow,

off into the wilds where the girls are screaming, wanting
his babies, no questions asked, ah yes, the subtle grass
of the wilds, and the drum-beat of the human heart.

V
GRACELAND

FLYING TO MEMPHIS

The child in the seat next to me says
her doll's named Maggie Mae, which puts me
in a red haze, thinking of Rod Stewart—
his wild old Maggie seducing him from school,

while this primly propped doll's owner struggles
to read "African Water Buffaloes" in the airline
magazine. "You know what *extinct* means,
don't you?" her father asks. "Gone forever,"

she says. I am scratching my ear, sailing
like Peter Pan through my pre-TV,
pre-rock & roll silent sky. Feeling
the jolt of Stewart bringing his metallic voice

into it, his lurid red lights. I close
my eyes, sing in my head Bobby Vee's
Take Good Care of My Baby.
I do Paul Simon—"the Mississippi Delta's

shining like a National guitar." Memphis
slides under me, a galaxy of stars. I land South
with Simon, who's taking his son to Graceland,
the child of a former marriage. Who doesn't

need grace? You think you're going along,
a nice child, if quiet. Then the beat picks up.

2

LIP-SYNCHING

The same night, which is day in England,
crowds are laying flowers outside Westminster
Cathedral for Princess Di's funeral.
"It is Márgarét you mourn for," Hopkins said,

marking Márgarét as three syllables, a strangeness
that delights me still, as in the Richie Valens
song, "Oh Donna," that everyone knows
has to diphthong off the *o* in Donna, or if they don't

know, they ought to. My mind swings this way,
hungrily, cue to cue, headed backwards,
dying to fall into my delicious body
again. Donna. Oh, it's Donna Truax

and Jacqui Brandli, carrying their 45s
in cases down Garland Street to my house
where we would lip-synch to Richie and Elvis
and others, using our fists for a mike,

making hungry, misunderstood Elvis eyes,
no matter whose song—since Dion, Anka,
Avalon, all the Italian boys, even white-boy
Ricky, came together in the King—

until the awkward ecstasy would have us
pairing up under a blanket, kissing
and circling a finger on the bud of each other's
breasts while the third kept watch at the door.

3

THE HOUSE ON GARLAND STREET

The house on Garland Street cried out
like the house in Lawrence's "The Rocking Horse Winner,"
there must be more love, there must be more money,
there must be more. . .and my heart raced

into the four-four song of its own unhappiness,
pleased in a sour, peculiar way
by the abundance of longing, of shame, the drive
of it, by the kitchen precarious with dirty

dishes, our own spaghetti marooned
on the bowls, our own sticky spoons.

4

DRIVEWAY TO GRACELAND

Desire's built of granite blocks, though
you come to it softly: winding green approach
meant to ease you through to antebellum
grace, to Georgian columns, to when

a person could straighten her back, could
just breathe. Before anyone has thought
of war, before the husband comes home
drunk for the first time, hitting the wife.

Before that, maybe, before the moment
of absolute conviction that this is not love,
after all. Before I smoked my first Salem.
Before that, when I played in the creek

along the Wabash tracks, maybe, or scooped
moss from Nana's fishpond. Even these
scenes smolder, though, with grief that may
belong to my parents, Tara already burnt

to the ground. When I get to the actual ashes,
my stomach turns granite, nothing gets in.

5

ENTRANCE

"You've always wanted to be here, ladies
and gentlemen," says Melvin the bus driver,
"and now you're here." "The Wonder of You"
plays overhead. The sign says leave

your camera outside. Like the boy in Faulkner's
"The Bear," I put away my weapon
so the Once-Upon-a-Time can rear up in my face.
Sometimes the mind wants to take everything

Sunday-go-to-meeting seriously, to bow
like a good Episcopalian to the acetate records,
to live in our mutual thoughts the way
we lived in the songs. Other times a giggle

starts up, a sly escape. We're ushered
between the twin plaster lions at the door. Lovely,
lovely. I'm a guest in my own life, keeping
my mouth shut. Nothing about me is me.

LIVING ROOM

1957

And then Mrs. Moore, neé Brown, the previous
owner, divorced the doctor and sold her
mansion to the Presleys from the projects. Came
to have tea one afternoon shortly thereafter

with Mrs. Gladys Presley, neé Smith, formerly
of Tupelo, Mississippi, in what had once been
her formal parlor, done in oyster-white
and delicate pastels, with ancestral mirrors

on either side of the fireplace. There was wall-to-wall
carpet now, of a deep claret red—
just like what Scarlett O'Hara had
in her terrible Georgia mansion. Deep blue walls,

gold-painted moldings just below the ceiling,
brand new custom-made furniture—big stuff:
a fifteen-foot sofa and cocktail table
to match. The ladies enjoyed each other's

company. Mrs. Presley gave Mrs. Moore
the grand tour after tea. Mrs. Moore
especially admired the fully equipped
soda fountain and jukebox in the basement.

1997

Even though I have stepped inside his head,
now, the everyday Elvis barely looks up
from the TV, trying not to spill Coke
on the long white sofa. Eight friends could fit

on it and watch themselves being friends
in the marbled mirror-walls facing each other
across the room. Out of one eye, Elvis
watches Elvis sitting in the room that came

from Goldsmith's Furniture on Poplar Street.
He does not put his feet on the vast glass
coffee table, nor does he leave Coke rings.
He sits inside this life, careful

to keep the old one from doing anything
crude. His birthplace house, as he likes
to point out, could easily fit inside
this room. *Build thee more stately mansions,*
                                    O my soul

                        comes to me, not being Elvis,
only walking around inside his head,
held back by the museum ropes and my own

mind's eye, in which, at a remove, my mother
is wiping spilled juice from our plastic sofa
with wrought-iron legs. Juice has fallen
on the braided rug. The little Zenith TV

looks away, catches the picture window
with shadowbox squares. On the squares sit
what bric-a-brac we have to show, Nana's
cast-off alabaster parrots with broken tails,

the blue glass vase, a house in a globe
that snows when you turn it upside down.
My mother, Blanche DuBois in *Streetcar
Named Desire*, wipes, dazed, in a kind of

beauty, her old white-sofa life tucked
inside this one forever, while I am desperately
cleaning, stacking *Life, Time*, last week's
newspapers no one will throw away.

ELVIS'S BEDROOM

They have a velvet rope across the stairs.
I have to leave him alone up there,
dreaming trompe l'oeil clouds on the hallway
ceiling, dreaming his bedroom blue,

"the darkest blue there is," dreaming black
furniture. Leave him in his midnight with Jesus
on the easel by his bed; pass by the upper
landing, raised like hairs on my neck,

like a few bars of music climbing
and dissolving in front of me. Leave him with his
sleep mask on, windows blacked out.
Leave him in his giant quiet, his woman

or no woman, his restless sheets. Go on
with my tour, go on convincing myself
that if I were allowed upstairs, I'd retrieve
years of my life, that I could walk in

on the years so quietly they'd let me sit down
and think how to live with their hard facts.

THE KITCHEN

"Hi Honey, I'm home." In this scene,
a man takes off his hat, takes the *Times*
out of the dog's mouth, heads for the steel-clad
kitchen, heart of the home we all

craved—Elvis, June, Harriet, you, me,
all of us staring like tourists at the clueless
coppertone, hoping for a glimpse
of the heart, any sensation of heart. Heart

of Elvis, fat-and-starved on junk food.
Heart of our own fat-and-starved mothers,
spreading meringue on lemon pie. How light,
my mother's knife on the meringue, as if life

were not all that difficult! In the next scene,
I arrange a slice of my own pie on the plate
as if *Better Homes and Gardens* were coming
to photograph. *This way, not the way*

she used to do it, not ending that way,
in the kitchen after dinner, she sitting
on the countertop, their talk merged to a single
baffled will, a loose animal among

the hopeless appliances. This could happen
in Elvis's or any kitchen, even if
two people had tried to eat carefully,
minimizing the jolt to the system of taking

anything like love in. They might not
notice their small daughter spitting her peas
into the wastebasket, unable to eat at all.

LISA MARIE'S FAVORITE CHAIR

Lisa Marie Presley spits her peas
into the wastebasket, knots up like a pea
in the fruitwood jungle chair, "so big that a window
had to be removed to bring it in,"

Priscilla says on the tape. I know
how she curls to abandon the world, the kitchen
voices. How you climb down the chambered nautilus
of yourself, room after room. How the first dream

you have is a flicker of light on a curve.
You could name it Michael Jackson because
it is a cool dancer, pale-faced, androgynous:
perfect mother and father, not

breaking plates in the kitchen. You watch
your supposed love-light dance, refuse
to be caught, flare cold as panther eyes. In your future
of dreams he breaks free from a dense upholstery

of jungle leaves. You can never touch him.
Your factual life diverts, trying. You think
you're going straight but, then again, you're here.

THE JUNGLE ROOM

What's money for, if not to buy
the moment's furniture? You never know,
though, which regrettable colors and postures
will freeze in place: Tahitian tables

of distressed myrtlewood under thick polyurethane
forever. Matching jungle fronds on massive
drapes and chairs. The trapped breath
of the jungle, dead Elvis's Spot of Time,

like the one Wordsworth kept to himself
thirty years before he wrote *The Prelude*—
low breathings of the Alps down his neck.
I'm saying I wanted those terrible breathings

like I wanted to live, the dark breath
on my neck—the extremity of a stripped-down
Ford, The Big Bopper, maybe, singing "Oh baby,
you know what I like."
                                          "You'll marry him,"

my next-door neighbor Gail said,
fixing her lipstick, and she was right.
There I am, petrified in that old dazzled air,
one foot raised to step into the Ford
with a bedspread for upholstery—the moment
I stop breathing and can't move on.

THE MIRRORED STAIRWELL

There she is, dozens of her in unison,
stepping down to Elvis's basement pool room,
stepping through her multiple facets down
to the original, who is stepping onto the now-extinct

running board and into the Ford forever,
not dancing to the radio but climbing in
deliberate as an old woman, gathering her skirt
before the age of jeans, gathering herself

for the long sleep of sex, the ragged
lawns of Garland Street strewn behind her,
the music inside the houses stuck
the way music stays with the insane,

or people with Alzheimer's: "Mack the Knife,"
"Venus," "Lavender Blue," "Teenager
in Love," "Come Softly to Me," and so on.
Beyond the Ozark mountains, Alaska and Hawaii

become states. Nixon debates Khrushchev,
Castro takes over in Cuba. She steps
into the car as if into church, the closed eyes
of the center, the dark from which things wake,

if they can, if they sense the slightest break.

THE TROPHY ROOM

I'm trying to read the solid gold labels
of songs too hard to hear: Midas-touched,
fastened to plaques, encased in glass.
I'm walking through, being cool,

a flexible saxophone following along
inside my moments like genes in my cells.
I am shoulder-to-shoulder with a hundred tourists
mostly playing it cool—carrying the songs

as best they can themselves, xxjustified
in the dumb lyrics, in the ordinary tunes,
gold as they damned well ought to be,
and sacred as any other, entranced

by their own turning. I remember any
one scene in my life and it makes me smile
into a pothole of sadness, as if at the moment
of remembering I leave behind that scene

for tourists to stumble on stupidly, to try
stupidly to relate to their own lives.
In the overhead photo, Elvis is sneering,
detached as ever, one of the dubious

advantages of fame. Spun away from himself,
he collects himself on the walls, three rooms
of gold records, a "waterfall of gold
down the walls," a one-armed tourist says.

Elvis and I stare through glass at each other,
reflected back at ourselves. The air
between us burns in its old terrible way,
burns with the friction of a hundred tunes.

What were we thinking? What private
language did we think we had, that would hold
us together forever? Everybody comes here,
second only to the White House in visitors

per year. Ho hum, I thought the songs
were for me. I thought we could get along.

13

THE MEDITATION GARDEN

You're supposed to think on something
by the curved brick wall with Spanish
windows, cupping the two steps down
through Roman columns to the graves

where Elvis, Grandma, Vernon, Gladys,
and Jesse's little marker fan out
like bracelet charms below. Signs
of presences stand everywhere. Jesus

stretches out his arms to St. Francis
in cowl and hood, to a black river goddess
and a white one with an Elvis nose.
Cherubs bow their wings. A naked

blackened angel holds an empty pot
beneath his arm. No one knows
what lives inside the hollows of this world,
lip-synching from the other one.

Might as well include a pantheon
of gods, the whole shebang, just in case.
No sign's trivial: *Aaron's* engraved
with double *a*'s on Elvis's grave.

If he were really dead and buried,
the story goes, wouldn't they
have spelled it right—with just one *a*?
Didn't I believe Whitman when he said

"look for me beneath the soles of your feet?
Didn't I believe the former husband
who said "I'll haunt you forever"? But one
positive note: I've kept singing the old

songs in my lousy voice until they don't
even recognize themselves. And who's
to say who's right, with all the cover
versions since? Whose song

would you say "Blue Suede Shoes" is,
for instance, Carl Perkins's or Elvis's?

NOTES

In the poem "Living Room" on page 56, the section entitled "1957" is adapted from *Graceland* by Karal Ann Marling (Cambridge: Harvard University Press), 1996.

SOME RECENT TITLES IN THE CARNEGIE MELLON POETRY SERIES

1993
Trumpeter, Jeannine Savard
Cuba, Ricardo Pau-Llosa
The Night World and the Word Night, Franz Wright
The Book of Complaints, Richard Katrovas

1994
If Winter Come: Collected Poems, 1967–1992, Alvin Aubert
Of Desire and Disorder, Wayne Dodd
Ungodliness, Leslie Adrienne Miller
Rain, Henry Carlile
Windows, Jay Meek
A Handful of Bees, Dzvinia Orlowsky

1995
Germany, Caroline Finkelstein
Housekeeping in a Dream, Laura Kasischke
About Distance, Gregory Djanikian
Wind of the White Dresses, Mekeel McBride
Above the Tree Line, Kathy Mangan
In the Country of Elegies, T. Alan Broughton
Scenes from the Light Years, Anne C. Bromley
Quartet, Angela Ball
Rorschach Test, Franz Wright

1996
Back Roads, Patricia Henley
Dyer's Thistle, Peter Balakian
Beckon, Gillian Conoley
The Parable of Fire, James Reiss
Cold Pluto, Mary Ruefle
Orders of Affection, Arthur Smith
Colander, Michael McFee

1997

Growing Darkness, Growing Light, Jean Valentine
Selected Poems, 1965-1995, Michael Dennis Browne
Your Rightful Childhood: New and Selected Poems, Paula Rankin
Headlands: New and Selected Poems, Jay Meek
Soul Train, Allison Joseph
The Autobiography of a Jukebox, Cornelius Eady
The Patience of the Cloud Photographer, Elizabeth Holmes
Madly in Love, Aliki Barnstone
An Octave Above Thunder: New and Selected Poems, Carol Muske

1998

Yesterday Had a Man In It, Leslie Adrienne Miller
Definition of the Soul, John Skoyles
Dithyrambs, Richard Katrovas
Postal Routes, Elizabeth Kirschner
The Blue Salvages, Wayne Dodd
The Joy Addict, James Harms
Clemency and Other Poems, Colette Inez
Scattering the Ashes, Jeff Friedman
Sacred Conversations, Peter Cooley
Life Among the Trolls, Maura Stanton

1999

Justice, Caroline Finkelstein
Edge of House, Dzvinia Orlowsky
A Thousand Friends of Rain: New and Selected Poems, 1976-1998,
    Kim Stafford
The Devil's Child, Fleda Brown Jackson
World as Dictionary, Jesse Lee Kercheval
Vereda Tropical, Ricardo Pau-Llosa
The Museum of the Revolution, Angela Ball
Our Master Plan, Dara Wier

2000

Small Boat with Oars of Different Size, Thom Ward
Post Meridian, Mary Ruefle

Hierarchies of Rue, Roger Sauls
Constant Longing, Dennis Sampson
Mortal Education, Joyce Peseroff
How Things Are, James Richardson
Years Later, Gregory Djanikian
On the Waterbed They Sank to Their Own Levels, Sarah Rosenblatt
Blue Jesus, Jim Daniels
Winter Morning Walks: 100 Postcards to Jim Harrison, Ted Kooser

2001
The Deepest Part of the River, Mekeel McBride
The Origin of Green, T. Alan Broughton
Day Moon, Jon Anderson
Glacier Wine, Maura Stanton
Earthly, Michael McFee
Lovers in the Used World, Gillian Conoley
Sex Lives of the Poor and Obscure, David Schloss
Voyages in English, Dara Wier
Quarters, James Harms
Mastodon, 80% Complete, Jonathan Johnson
Ten Thousand Good Mornings, James Reiss
The World's Last Night, Margot Schilpp

2002
Astronaut, Brian Henry
Among the Musk Ox People, Mary Ruefle
The Finger Bone, Kevin Prufer
Keeping Time, Suzanne Cleary
From the Book of Changes, Stephen Tapscott
What it Wasn't, Laura Kasischke
The Late World, Arthur Smith
Slow Risen Among the Smoke Trees, Elizabeth Kirschner

2003
Imitation of Life, Allison Joseph
A Place Made of Starlight, Peter Cooley
The Mastery Impulse, Ricardo Pau-Llosa

Except for One Obscene Brushstroke, Dzvinia Orlowsky
Taking Down the Angel, Jeff Friedman
Casino of the Sun, Jerry Williams
Trouble, Mary Baine Campbell
Lives of Water, John Hoppenthaler

2004
Freeways and Aqueducts, James Harms
Tristimania, Mary Ruefle
Prague Winter, Richard Katrovas
Venus Examines Her Breast, Maureen Seaton
Trains in Winter, Jay Meek
The Women Who Loved Elvis All Their Lives, Fleda Brown
The Chronic Liar Buys a Canary, Elizabeth Edwards
Various Orbits, Thom Ward